ESSENTIAL ELEMENTS

PIANO THEORY

T0066153

ISBN 978-1-4950-5732-8

7777 W. BLUEMOUND RD. P.O. BOX 13819 MILWAUKEE, WI 53213

In Australia Contact:
Hal Leonard Australia Pty. Ltd.
4 Lentara Court
Cheltenham, Victoria, 3192 Australia
Email: ausadmin@halleonard.com.au

Visit Hal Leonard Online at
www.halleonard.com

To the Student

I wrote these books with you in mind. As a young student I often wondered how completing theory work-books would make me a better musician. The theory work often seemed separate from the music I was play-ing. My goal in *Essential Elements Piano Theory* is to provide you with the tools you will need to compose, improvise, play classical and popular music, or to better understand any other musical pursuit you might en-joy. In each "Musical Mastery" section of this book you will experience creative applications of the theory you have learned. The "Ear Training" pages will be completed with your teacher at the lesson. In this series you will begin to learn the building blocks of music, which make it possible for you to have fun at the piano. A practical understanding of theory enables you to see what is possible in music. I wish you all the best on your journey as you learn the language of music!

Sincerely,
Mona Rejino

To the Teacher

I believe that knowledge of theory is most beneficial when a concept is followed directly by a musical application. In *Essential Elements Piano Theory*, learning theory becomes far more than completing worksheets. Students have the opportunity to see why learning a particular concept can help them become a better pianist right away. They can also see how the knowledge of musical patterns and chord progressions will enable them to be creative in their own musical pursuits: composing, arrang-ing, improvising, playing classical and popular music, accompanying, or any other.

A free download of the *Teacher's Answer Key* is available at www.halleonard.com/eeptheory8answer.

Acknowledgements

I would like to thank Hal Leonard LLC for providing me the opportunity to put these theoretical thoughts down on paper and share them with others. I owe a debt of gratitude to Jennifer Linn, who has helped with this project every step of the way. These books would not have been possible with-out the support of my family: To my husband, Richard, for his wisdom and amazing ability to solve dilemmas; to my children, Maggie and Adam, for helping me think outside the box.

TABLE OF CONTENTS

REVIEW

1. Add bar lines to each rhythm below.

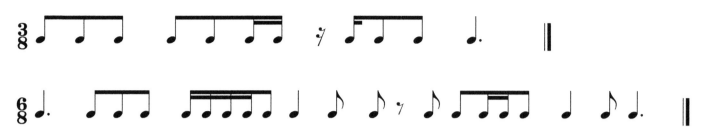

2. Fill in the blank with the correct meter for each measure: Simple, Compound or Asymmetrical

_____   _____   _____   _____

3. Complete the linear Circle of Fifths for minor keys.

Down by Perfect 5ths ◄——————————   ——————————► Up by Perfect 5ths

a

4. Name each Major key signature and its relative minor key signature.

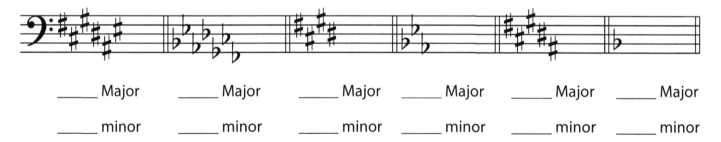

_____ Major   _____ Major   _____ Major   _____ Major   _____ Major   _____ Major

_____ minor   _____ minor   _____ minor   _____ minor   _____ minor   _____ minor

5. Draw the minor key signature named below each measure.

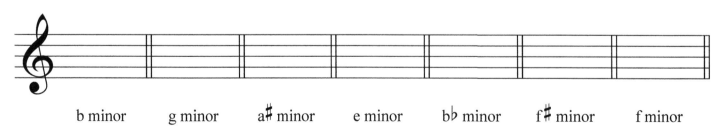

b minor   g minor   a# minor   e minor   b♭ minor   f# minor   f minor

6. Add accidentals to complete the following scales.

a Melodic Minor

b♭ Harmonic Minor

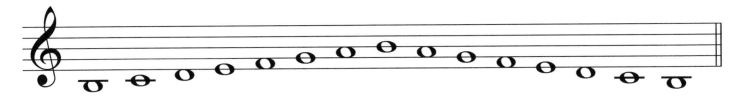

d♯ Natural Minor

7. Fill in the blanks.

   a. Major intervals of the scale become _____ intervals when the upper note is lowered a half step.

   b. Perfect and Major intervals of the scale become _____ intervals when the upper note is raised a half step.

   c. Perfect and minor intervals become _____ intervals when the upper note is lowered a half step.

8. Identify each interval by type (P, M, m, Aug or dim) and size.

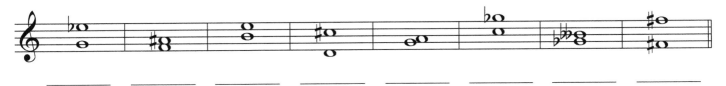

9. Label the question and answer phrases by filling in the blanks.

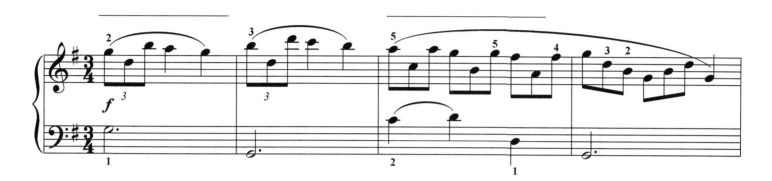

10. Label the motive and sequence by filling in the blanks.

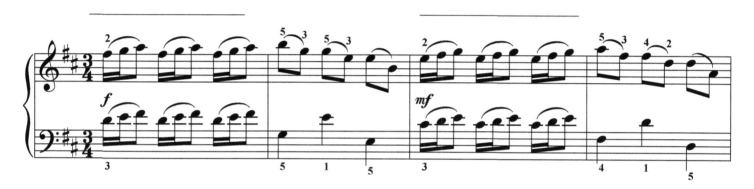

11. Label the motive and repetition by filling in the blanks.

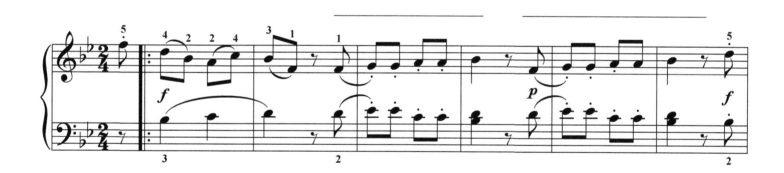

12. Label the motive and imitation by filling in the blanks.

Triads of the Scale

Triads built on the 1st, 4th and 5th notes of a Major scale are called **PRIMARY TRIADS**. Triads built on the 2nd, 3rd, 6th and 7th notes of a Major scale are called **SECONDARY TRIADS**.

In Major keys, the I, IV and V chords are Major. The ii, iii and vi chords are minor, and the vii° chord is diminished.

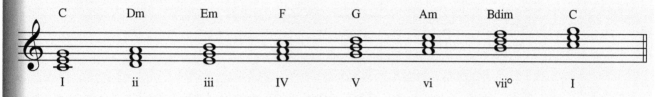

1. Label each triad in the given key by placing Roman numerals below and letter names above. Play each chord.

D Major

F Major

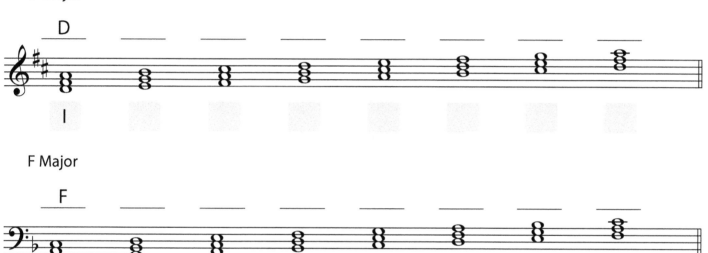

2. Draw the triads of the B♭ Major scale. Place Roman numerals below and letter names above each triad. Play each chord.

B♭ Major

Triads built on the 1st, 4th and 5th notes of a minor scale are **PRIMARY TRIADS**. Triads built on the 2nd, 3rd, 6th and 7th notes of a minor scale are **SECONDARY TRIADS**.

In minor keys, the triads are either Major, minor, Augmented or diminished.

a Harmonic Minor

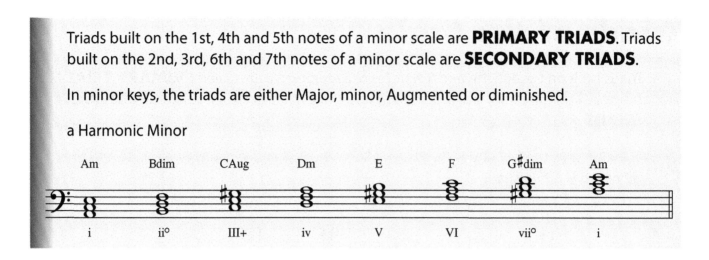

3. Identify each triad in the given key by placing Roman numerals below and letter names above. Play each chord.

g Harmonic Minor

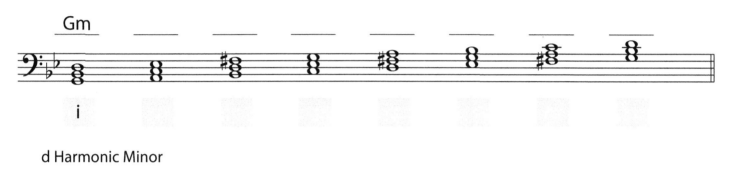

d Harmonic Minor

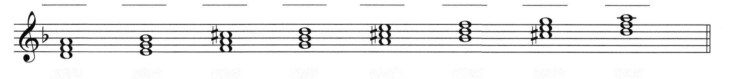

4. Draw the triads of the e harmonic minor scale. Remember to add the necessary accidentals. Play each chord.

e Harmonic Minor

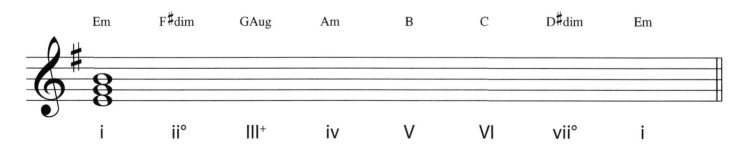

Each **SCALE DEGREE** has a name in both Major and minor keys.

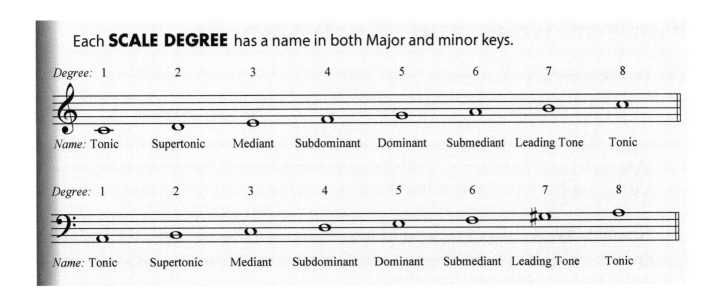

5. Fill in the blanks.

   a. Names for the Primary Triads are tonic, _____ and _____.

   b. Names for the Secondary Triads are supertonic, _____ ,

   _____ , and _____ _____ .

6. Circle the number for each of the following scale degree names.

   a. Dominant: 1   5   7

   b. Supertonic: 2   3   6

   c. Leading Tone: 3   4   7

   d. Submediant: 2   3   6

   e. Tonic: 1   4   5

   f. Mediant: 2   3   7

   g. Subdominant: 1   2   4

Figured Bass and Slash Chords

TRIADS have three positions.

Root Position	First Inversion	Second Inversion
root is the lowest note	3rd is the lowest note	5th is the lowest note

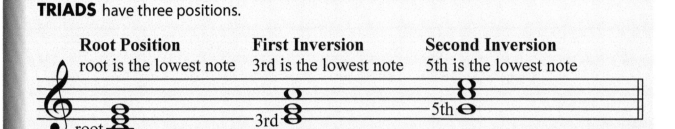

FIGURED BASS is a type of musical shorthand used to indicate the position of a chord. Arabic numerals identify the intervals above the lowest note. This system was widely used during the Baroque Period (1600-1750).

Key of C Major

A **root position triad** has intervals of a 5th and a 3rd.

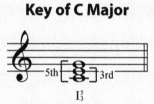

A **first inversion triad** has intervals of a 6th and a 3rd.

A **second inversion triad** has intervals of a 6th and a 4th.

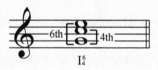

1. Circle the figured bass that matches each triad. *The first one is done for you.*

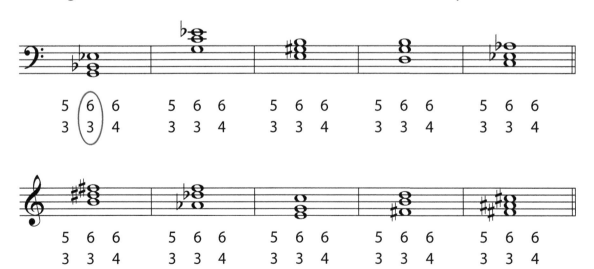

Usually, root position chords are indicated by Roman numeral only, and the numbers are omitted. In first inversion chords, the number 3 is generally omitted.

$$\text{I}_3^5 = \text{I} \qquad \text{I}_3^6 = \text{I}^6$$

2. Follow the examples given and write the figured bass for these chords.

Key of D Major

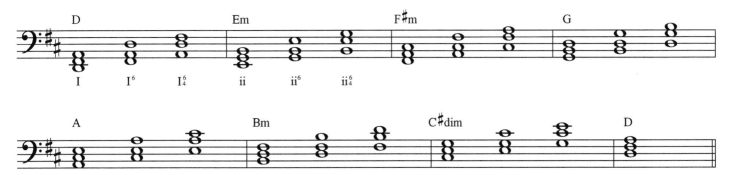

3. Complete a first inversion triad above each note. Play the chords.

Key of A Major

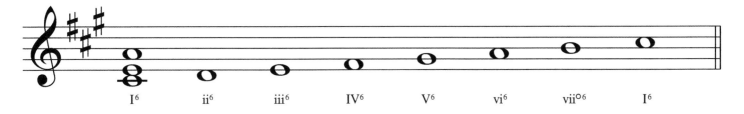

4. Complete a second inversion triad above each note. Play the chords.

Key of F Major

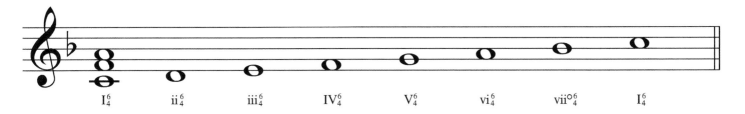

Another way to indicate 1st inversion and 2nd inversion triads is through the use of slash chords, especially in jazz and popular music. A **SLASH CHORD** is formed when a chord symbol is followed by a bass note that is different from the root of the chord.

G/B indicates a 1st inversion G Major chord with B as the lowest note.

G/D indicates a 2nd inversion G Major chord with D as the lowest note.

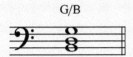 

5. Fill in the root note. Write the slash chord to identify each triad. *The first two are done for you.*

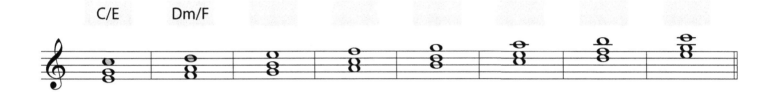

Figured Bass for Dominant Seventh Chords

A **DOMINANT SEVENTH CHORD** has three inversions. It can be inverted so that the third, fifth or seventh of the chord becomes the lowest note. In each inversion, the root is the top note of the interval of a second.

Key of C (Major or minor)

Root Position	1st Inversion	2nd Inversion	3rd Inversion
G7	G7/B	G7/D	G7/F

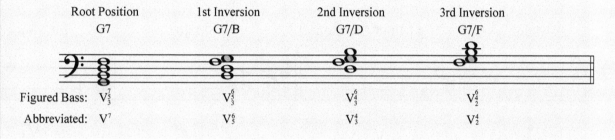

	Root Position	1st Inversion	2nd Inversion	3rd Inversion
Figured Bass:	V^7_3	V^6_5	V^6_4	V^6_4
Abbreviated:	V^7	V^6_5	V^4_3	V^4_2

1. Fill in the root note. Name each dominant seventh chord using the abbreviated figured bass shown above. *The first one is done for you.*

Key of G Major

Key of B♭ Major

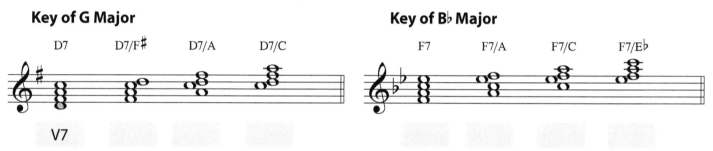

V7

2. Identify each dominant seventh chord by writing the letter name above and the abbreviated figured bass below. *The first one is done for you.*

Key of E Major

Key of d minor (Harmonic)

B7/F♯

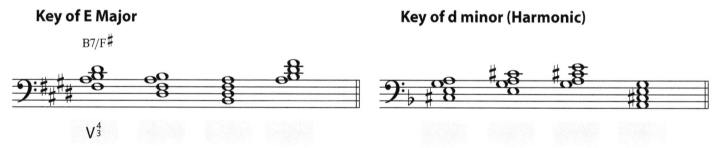

V^4_3

3. Name the Major key to which each of these dominant seventh chords belongs. *Count down a Perfect 5th from the root.*

Key of: _____ Major _____ Major _____ Major _____ Major

4. Write the following dominant seventh chords in the given key.

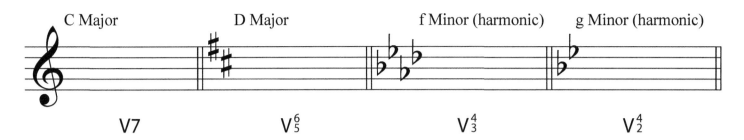

C Major	D Major	f Minor (harmonic)	g Minor (harmonic)
$V7$	V^6_5	V^4_3	V^4_2

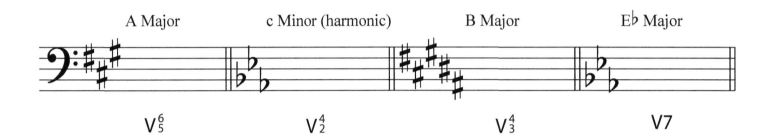

A Major	c Minor (harmonic)	B Major	E♭ Major
V^6_5	V^4_2	V^4_3	$V7$

5. Three chords are missing in each chord progression. Draw the missing chords on the staff using the figured bass and chord symbols as a guide. Play each chord progression.

G Major

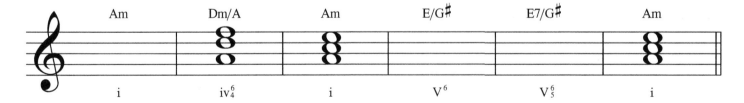

G	C/G	G	D/F♯	D7/F♯	G
I	IV^6_4	I	V^6	V^6_5	I

a Minor (Harmonic)

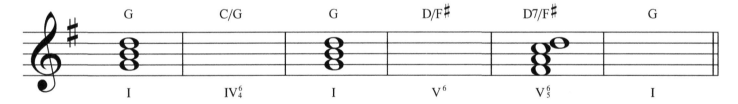

Am	Dm/A	Am	E/G♯	E7/G♯	Am
i	iv^6_4	i	V^6	V^6_5	i

B♭ Major

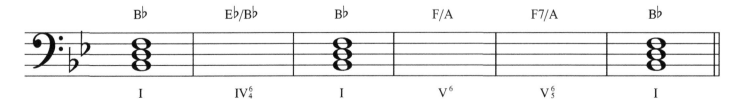

B♭	E♭/B♭	B♭	F/A	F7/A	B♭
I	IV^6_4	I	V^6	V^6_5	I

MUSICAL MASTERY

Ear Training

1. You will hear eight measures of melodic dictation. Fill in the blank measures with the notes and rhythms you hear. *The last note of measure 4 will end on the dominant, and measure 8 will end on the tonic.*

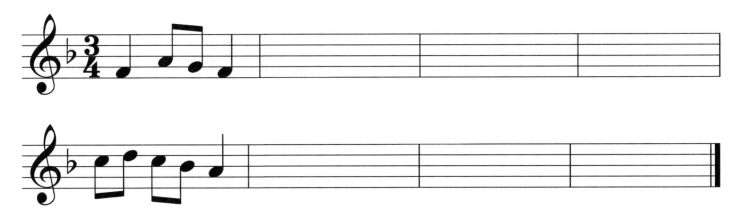

2. You will hear intervals of a Major 2nd, Major 3rd, Major 6th or Major 7th played in broken and blocked form. Name the correct interval in each blank.

   1. _____   2. _____   3. _____

   4. _____   5. _____   6. _____

3. You will hear intervals of a minor 2nd, minor 3rd, minor 6th or minor 7th played in broken and blocked form. Name the correct interval in each blank.

   1. _____   2. _____   3. _____

   4. _____   5. _____   6. _____

4. You will hear intervals of a Perfect unison, Perfect 4th, Perfect 5th or Perfect 8th played in broken and blocked form. Name the correct interval in each blank.

   1. _____   2. _____   3. _____

   4. _____   5. _____   6. _____

Lead Sheets

By using a combination of root position and slash chords (inversions), you can create smooth chord progressions in lead sheets.

1. The following left hand chords will be used in "Wayfaring Stranger": Em, Am/E, A/E and B7/D♯. Write these chords on the staff below. Practice them before adding the right hand melody. *You may omit the 5th in the B7/D♯ chord. The first one is done for you.*

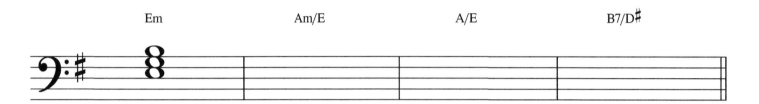

2. Combine the melody and chords to create your own arrangement.

Wayfaring Stranger

Spiritual

3. The following left hand chords will be used in "Shenandoah": F, B♭/F, Am/E, Dm, Gm/D, F/C, Am/C, B♭/D and C7/E. Write these chords on the staff below. Practice them before adding the right hand melody. *You may omit the 5th in the C7/E chord. The first one is done for you.*

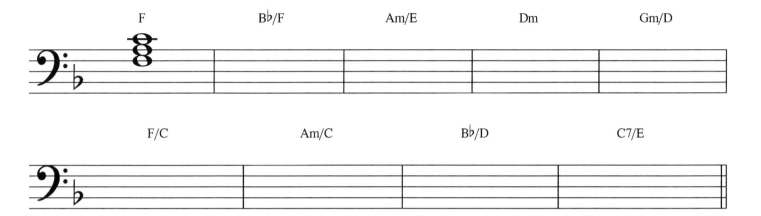

4. Combine the melody and chords to create your own arrangement.

Shenandoah

American Folksong

Parallel Major and Minor Keys and Scales

PARALLEL MAJOR and **MINOR KEYS** share the same tonic (key name), but have different key signatures.

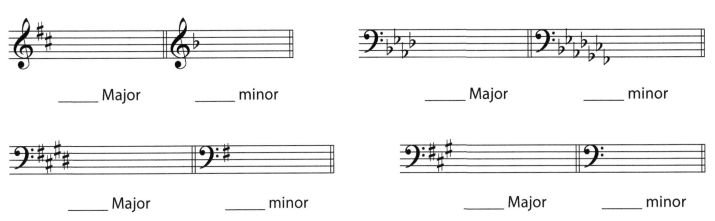

1. Name these parallel Major and minor keys.

_____ Major   _____ minor   _____ Major   _____ minor

_____ Major   _____ minor   _____ Major   _____ minor

2. Circle the correct word (relative or parallel) to complete each sentence.

   a. E♭ Major and e♭ minor are relative/parallel keys.

   b. B Major and b minor are relative/parallel keys.

   c. F Major and d minor are relative/parallel keys.

   d. F♯ Major and f♯ minor are relative/parallel keys.

   e. D Major and b minor are relative/parallel keys.

   f. C Major and a minor are relative/parallel keys.

3. Draw the parallel minor key signature for each Major key given.

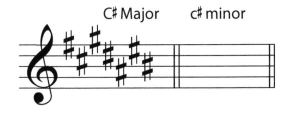

PARALLEL MAJOR and **MINOR SCALES** share the same tonic (keynote), but have different key signatures.

4. Draw the key signature for the following Major and parallel minor scales. After the key signature, draw the notes for each scale ascending. *The first one is done for you.*

G Major

g Harmonic minor

D Major

d Harmonic minor

C Major

c Harmonic minor

B♭ Major

b♭ Harmonic minor

A Major

a Harmonic minor

E Major

e Harmonic minor

Chromatic, Whole Tone and Blues Scales

A **CHROMATIC SCALE** consists of half steps in consecutive order. It has 12 tones and may begin on any note. An ascending chromatic scale uses sharp signs. A descending chromatic scale uses flat signs.

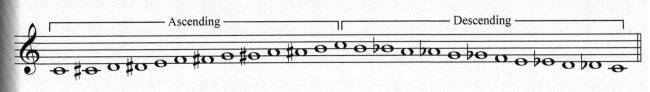

1. Complete the ascending chromatic scales by adding the necessary accidentals.

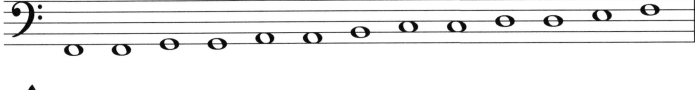

2. Complete the descending chromatic scales by adding the necessary accidentals.

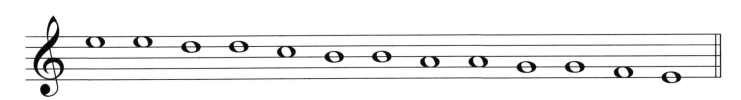

3. Write chromatic scales from the given note.

   Ascending

   Descending

A **WHOLE TONE SCALE** consists of whole steps in consecutive order. It has six tones and may begin on any note. An ascending whole tone scale uses sharp signs. A descending whole tone scale uses flat signs.

4. Complete the ascending whole tone scales by adding the necessary accidentals.

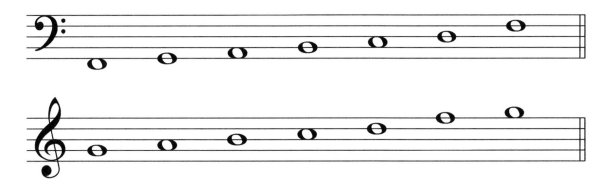

5. Complete the descending whole tone scales by adding the necessary accidentals.

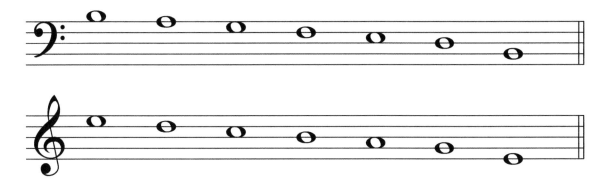

6. Write whole tone scales from the given note.

Ascending

Descending

A **BLUES SCALE** consists of six different tones and may begin on any note. To change a Major scale into a Blues scale, omit the 2nd and 6th scale degrees, flat (lower) the 3rd and 7th scale degrees and add a flatted (lowered) 5th.

C Major Scale

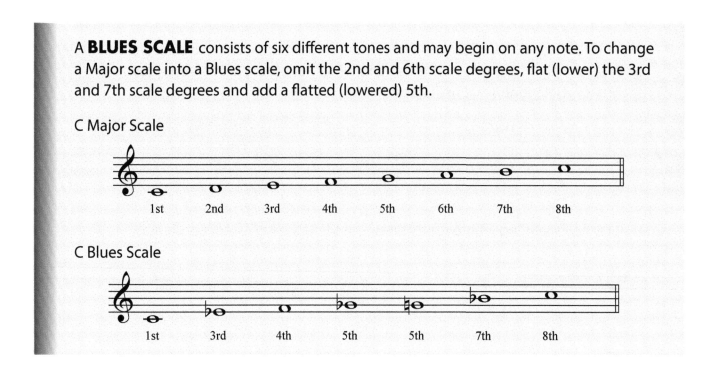

C Blues Scale

7. Complete the following blues scales by adding the necessary accidentals.

F Blues Scale

D Blues Scale

8. Write these blues scales from the given note.

G Blues Scale

A Blues Scale

Texture in Music

MUSICAL TEXTURE refers to the number and type of layers used in a composition, and how they relate to each other. In **POLYPHONIC** music, two or more melodic lines are played at the same time.

March from Notebook for Anna Magdalena Bach

Menuet en Rondeau by Rameau

In **HOMOPHONIC** music, a melody line is played in one hand and a chordal accompaniment is played in the other hand. The accompaniment may use blocked or broken chords.

Scherzo by von Weber

Sonatina Op. 36, No. 2 by Clementi

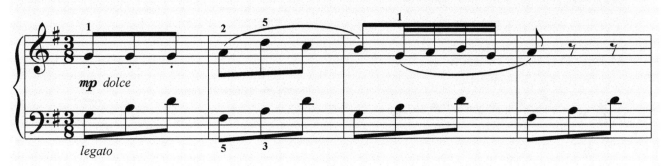

1. Name the texture used in each musical example below. Write polyphonic or homophonic in each blank.

Dance Intermezzo by Bertini _____

Bourée by Kirnberger _____

Sonatina in G by Attwood _____

The Merry Farmer by Schumann _____

Menuet in D Minor by Bach _____

Form in Music

MUSICAL FORM refers to the structure of a composition. It describes how the piece is divided into sections, and how they fit together. In **BINARY FORM**, there are two sections: **A** and **B**. Each section is usually repeated.

‖: A :‖ B :‖

Minuet

Alexander Reinagle
(1756-1809)

1. Label each section either A or B in the appropriate box.

2. Identify the question and answer phrases in the blanks.

In **TERNARY FORM**, there are three sections: **A**, **B**, and a repeat of **A**.

A   B   A

Sonatina in C Major

William Duncombe
(1690-1769)

3. Label each section either A or B in the appropriate box.

4. Identify the question and answer phrases in the blanks.

MUSICAL MASTERY

Ear Training

1. You will hear six scales ascending. Fill in the blank with the type of scale that you hear: Major, harmonic minor, chromatic, whole tone or blues.

   1. _____   2. _____   3. _____

   4. _____   5. _____   6. _____

2. You will hear two scales ascending in each group. The first scale is Major and the second scale is minor. Fill in the blank with the word that describes the relationship of those two scales: relative or parallel.

   1. _____   2. _____   3. _____

   4. _____   5. _____   6. _____

3. You will hear six triads played in broken and blocked form. Identify them as Major, minor, Augmented or diminished.

   1. _____   2. _____   3. _____

   4. _____   5. _____   6. _____

4. Listen to the texture of the following musical excerpts. Circle the word that describes what you hear.

   a. polyphonic   homophonic   b. polyphonic   homophonic

   c. polyphonic   homophonic   d. polyphonic   homophonic

Analysis

Study each musical example, then answer the questions about it.

Prelude, Op. 37 by Concone

1. Is the circled harmonic third Augmented, Major, minor or diminished? _____

2. Circle the correct figured bass to identify the circled triad: i, i⁶ or i⁶₄

3. What kind of scales are used? _____

Aquarium Dreams by Rejino

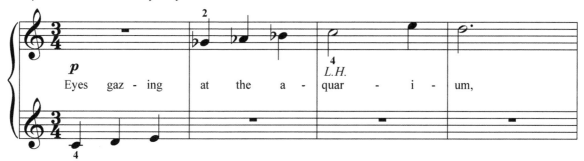

1. What type of meter is used?   simple   compound   asymmetrical

2. What kind of scales are used? _____

Late-Night Jazz by Rejino

1. Is the circled harmonic third Augmented, Major, minor or diminished? _____

2. What kind of scales are used? _____

Composing and Reading Mastery

1. Follow the directions to complete the right hand melody.

    a. In measure 1, continue writing an ascending chromatic scale in eighth notes.

    b. In measure 2, continue writing a descending chromatic scale in eighth notes.

    c. In measures 3 and 4, continue writing an ascending chromatic scale in eighth notes.

    d. Play the completed musical example.

2. Play the following 12–bar blues.

3. Place fingers 2, 3 and 4 of your left hand on a group of three black keys. Place fingers 2, 3 and 4 of your right hand on a C-D-E group. Depress the damper pedal. Explore patterns up and down the keyboard and create your own whole tone composition.

UNIT 9

Common Chord Progressions

Music written in **FOUR PART HARMONY** defines the complete harmonic structure of chords beyond the triad. In four part harmony, the bass voice (lowest note) determines whether the entire chord is in root position or is inverted.

1. Play the following I – IV – I_4^6 - V7 – I chord progression.

C Major

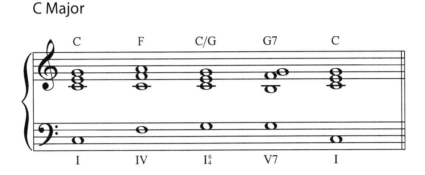

2. Write this chord progression in the given keys, following the example above. Begin with the bass voice, and look for common tones between the chords. Place chord symbols in the boxes, then play the progression.

F Major

D Major

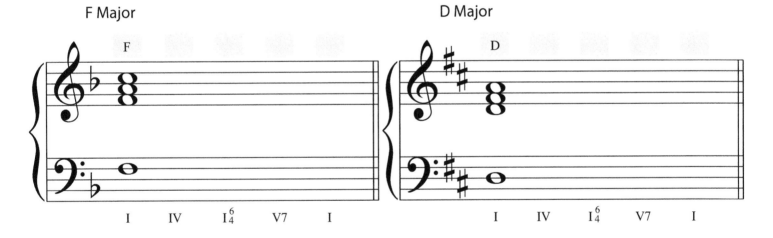

3. Play the following I – ii⁶ – I_4^6 - V7 - I chord progression.

C Major

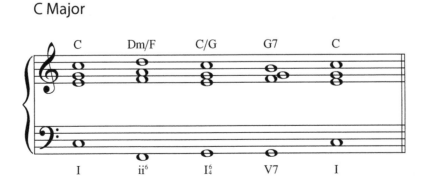

4. Write this chord progression in the given keys, following the previous example. Place figured bass in the boxes, then play the progression.

E♭ Major

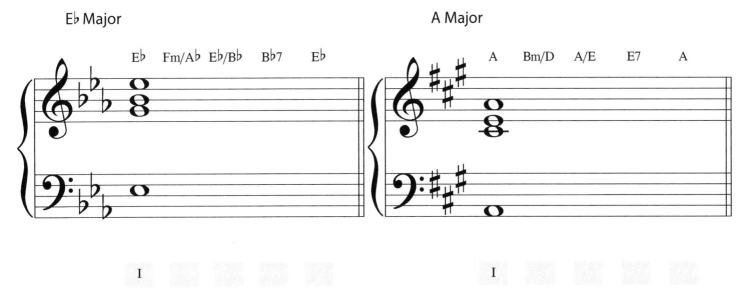

A Major

5. Play the following I – vi – IV – ii⁶ - I⁶₄ - V7 – I chord progression. Place the correct chord symbols in the boxes.

G Major

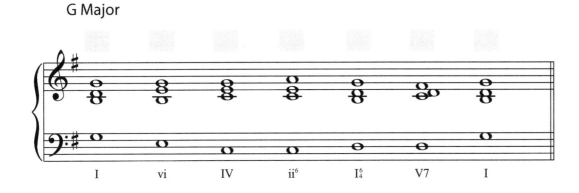

I	vi	IV	ii⁶	I⁶₄	V7	I

6. The I – vi – IV – V chord progression is often used in popular music. Play this progression in the Key of F Major. Write the progression in the other keys given, then play it.

F Major   B♭ Major   A Major

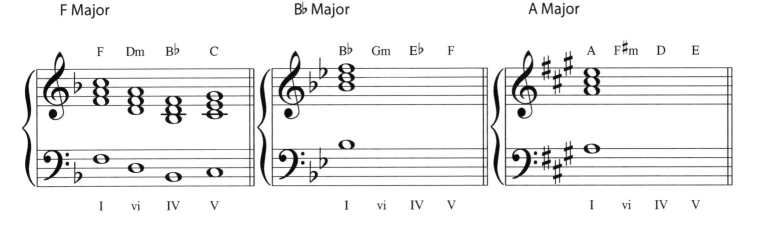

Harmonizing a Melody

To **HARMONIZE** a melody, you create a chordal accompaniment for it.

1. Play the melody.

2. Determine the key signature. The first and last notes of the melody will help you.

3. Practice the Primary Triads (I, IV, V7 or i, iv, V7) in that key. Use a combination of root position and inverted chords to create a smooth chord progression.

4. Analyze the melody to determine which chord tones match it.

5. Write the chord you chose in each box.

6. Combine the melody and accompaniment, and play the piece.

Melodies often include notes that are not part of the chord. Sometimes melodies step up or down from a chord tone, then immediately return to the same chord tone. These non-chord tones are called **UPPER NEIGHBORS** and **LOWER NEIGHBORS**.

7. Circle all of the upper neighbors and lower neighbors in "Grandfather's Clock." There are a total of four neighboring tones.

8. Follow the step by step directions on page 32 to harmonize "Grandfather's Clock."

Grandfather's Clock

Henry Clay Work

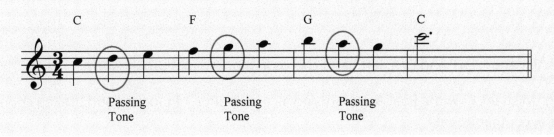

Sometimes a melody passes from one chord tone to a different chord tone in stepwise motion. These non-chord tones are called **PASSING TONES**.

9. Circle all of the passing tones in the music below. There are five passing tones.

10. Follow the directions on page 32 to harmonize the piece below.

Accompaniment Patterns

The following **ACCOMPANIMENT PATTERNS** are commonly found in music. When accompanying a melody, patterns often need to be varied depending on the chord progressions, harmonic rhythm and style of the piece.

1. Practice the F, B♭/F and C7/E left hand chords in blocked and broken form.

2. Play "Michael, Row the Boat Ashore" using a combination of blocked and broken chords for the accompaniment.

Michael, Row the Boat Ashore

Spiritual

3. Practice the D, B7/D♯, Em and A7/C♯ left hand chords in blocked and waltz bass style.

4. Play "Blow the Man Down" using a combination of blocked chords and waltz bass for the accompaniment.

Blow the Man Down

Traditional

5. Practice the E, Am/E and Dm left hand chords in jump bass style.

6. Play "Hava Nagila" using a jump bass accompaniment.

Hava Nagila

Israeli Folk Song

7. Practice the G/D, C/E, D7 and G chords in blocked and broken form.

8. Play "Amazing Grace" using a combination of these two accompaniment styles.

Amazing Grace

Traditional

9. Practice the Dm, C, F and A chords in blocked and jump bass style.

10. Play "Shalom Chaverim."

Shalom Chaverim

Israeli Folk Song

REVIEW

1. Fill in the blanks with the correct answer. Select from the terms in the box.

secondary	polyphonic	relative	chromatic
passing tones	submediant		binary
ternary	figured bass	mediant	primary
whole tone	supertonic	dominant seventh	
parallel	neighboring tones	slash chord	homophonic
blues	leading tone		

a. Triads built on the 2nd, 3rd, 6th and 7th notes of a scale are called _____ triads.

b. Scale degree three is called _____.

c. Scale degree seven is called _____ _____.

d. When a chord symbol is followed by a bass note that is different from its root, it is called a

 _____ _____.

e. A type of musical shorthand that indicates the position of a chord is called

 _____ _____.

f. A _____ _____ chord has three inversions.

g. Major and minor keys that share the same tonic are called _____.

h. A _____ scale is made up of half steps only.

i. At least two melodic lines are played at the same time in _____ music.

j. There are two sections of music in _____ form.

k. Non-chord tones that step up or down, then immediately return to the same chord tone are

 called _____ _____.

2. Draw the root position triads of the G Major scale. Place Roman numerals below each triad.

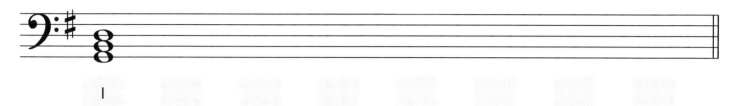

I

3. Draw the root position triads of the b harmonic minor scale, adding the necessary accidentals. Place Roman numerals below each triad.

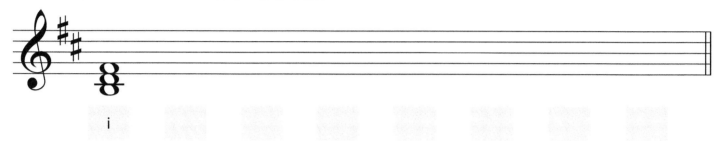

i

4. Draw a line connecting the triad or dominant seventh chord to its matching figured bass. All examples are in the Key of C Major.

I_4^6

I

I^6

V_5^6

V_2^4

V_3^4

V^7

5. Fill in the root note. Write a slash chord in each box to identify the triad. *The first one is done for you.*

Eb/Bb

6. Fill in the root note. Write the figured bass for each chord. *The first one is done for you.*

Key of Bb Major

ii^6

7. Draw the parallel minor key signature for each Major key given.

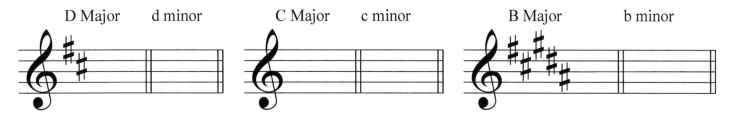

8. Fill in the blanks with the correct number for these parallel keys.

a. The key of G Major has 1 sharp. The key of g minor has _____ flat(s).

b. The key of E♭ Major has 3 flats. The key of e♭ minor has _____ flat(s).

c. The key of A Major has 3 sharps. The key of a minor has _____ sharp(s).

9. Draw the missing notes for each scale.

Chromatic (ascending)

Chromatic (descending)

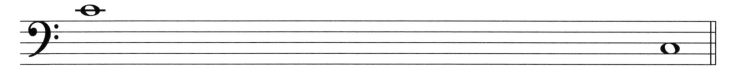

10. What types of scales are shown below?

11. Label the following circled notes as upper neighbor (u.n.), lower neighbor (l.n.) or passing tone (p.t.).

12. Binary form consists of two sections: _____ and _____. Ternary form consists of three sections: _____, _____ and _____.

13. Name the texture for each musical example.

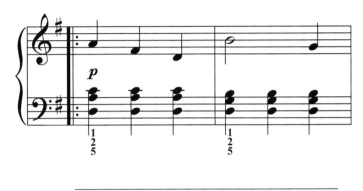 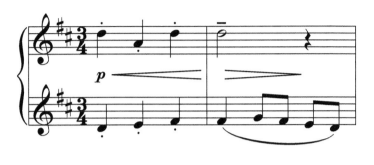

_____   _____

14. In the following chord progressions, place chord symbols in the boxes above each harmony. Place figured bass in the boxes below.

G Major

D Major

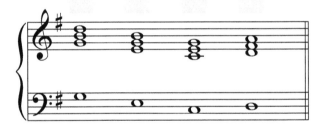 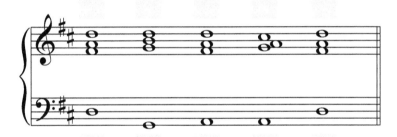

B♭ Major

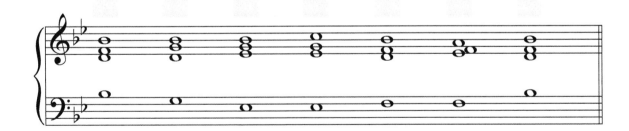

MUSICAL MASTERY

Ear Training

1. You will hear eight measures of melodic dictation. Fill in the blank measures with the notes and rhythms you hear.

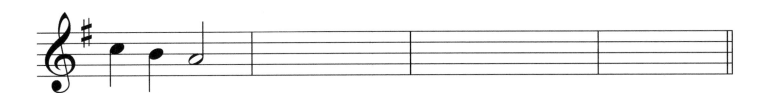

2. You will hear the following intervals played from the same root note in broken and blocked form: M2, M3, P4, P5, M6, M7 and P8. Name the interval by type and size.

   1. _____   2. _____   3. _____   4. _____   5. _____   6. _____

3. You will hear four measures of rhythmic dictation. Fill in the blank measures with the rhythm you hear.

4. One chord is missing from each chord progression. Listen for the missing triad and fill in the boxes with I, i, IV, iv or V7.

a.	i		i	V7
b.	I		I	IV
c.	I	V7		V7
d.	I	V7		I
e.		V7	i	iv
f.	i	iv		i

Analysis

Study "Russian Folk Song," then answer the questions about it.

Russian Folk Song Op. 107, No. 7

Ludwig van Beethoven
(1770-1827)

1. This piece uses _____ part harmony throughout.

2. What is the key signature? _____

3. Write the chord symbols in the boxes to identify each chord.

Improvisation Mastery

1. Play the I – vi – IV – V chord progression in your left hand in the key of C Major, as follows:

2. With your right hand, improvise a melody using notes from the C Major scale.

3. Combine the right hand and left hand parts.

4. Transpose the I – vi – IV – V chord progression and the scale to the keys of G Major and F Major, combining both parts to create more improvisations.

Johann Pachelbel (1653-1706) composed the famous "Canon in D." Although it was written centuries ago, the chord progression from this piece has been widely used in popular music in the 20th and 21st centuries.

5. Play the I – V – vi – iii – IV – I – IV – V chord progression in your left hand in the key of D Major, as follows:

6. With your right hand, improvise a melody using notes from the D Major scale. You may also create a short motive, and repeat it as a sequence.

7. Combine the right hand and left hand parts.

8. Transpose the I – V – vi – iii – IV – I – IV – V chord progression and the scale (motive and sequence) to the keys of C Major and G Major, and create more improvisations.

Accompaniment Mastery

1. Practice the left hand chords from "Greensleeves" in blocked, broken and waltz bass styles. All chords will be played in root position.

2. Play "Greensleeves" using a combination of these three accompaniment styles.

Greensleeves

English Folk Song

THEORY MASTERY

Review Test

1. Draw the primary triads in root position.

E♭ Major

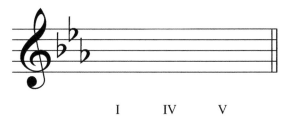

I   IV   V

Draw the secondary triads in root position.

A Major

ii   iii   vi   vii°

c♯ Minor (Harmonic)

i   iv   V

f Minor (Harmonic)

ii°   III+   VI   vii°

2. Determine the root note. Write the figured bass for each triad.

Key of D Major

3. Determine the root note. Write the figured bass for each dominant seventh chord.

Key of B♭ Major

Key of A minor (harmonic)

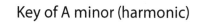

4. Draw the following slash chords.

C/E   Gm/D   F/A   E/B   B♭/F   D/F♯

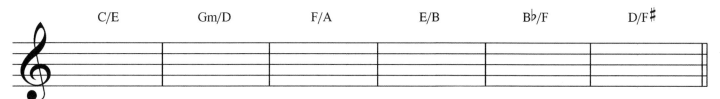

5. Draw the key signature for these parallel Major and harmonic minor scales. After the key signature, draw the notes for each scale ascending.

F Major   f Harmonic Minor

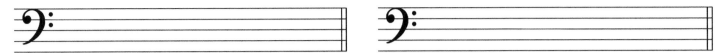

6. The following musical excerpts use common chord progressions. Write both the figured bass and the chord symbols in the boxes.

7. Harmonize the following melody using blocked chords in a smooth chord progression.

8. Write the letter of the correct definition in the blank beside each term.

_____ polyphonic

a. scale degree two

_____ whole tone scale

b. consists of half steps

_____ relative keys

c. two or more melodies played simultaneously

_____ supertonic

d. a piece having two sections, A and B

_____ non-chord tones

e. consists of whole steps

_____ chromatic scale

f. upper and lower neighbors

_____ binary form

g. share the same key signature

_____ subdominant

h. scale degree six

_____ accompaniments

i. structure of a composition

_____ homophonic

j. scale degree four

_____ submediant

k. blocked, broken, waltz and jump

_____ ternary form

l. has a flatted 3rd, 5th and 7th

_____ parallel keys

m. melody in one hand, chords in the other

_____ blues scale

n. a piece having three sections, A B A

_____ musical form

o. share the same tonic

Ear Training

1. You will hear three chord progressions. Circle the one you hear in each pair.

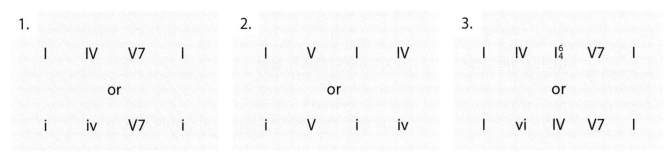

1.					2.					3.				
I	IV	V7	I		I	V	I	IV		I	IV	I$^6_4$	V7	I
	or					or					or			
i	iv	V7	i		i	V	i	iv		I	vi	IV	V7	I

2. You will hear six scales ascending. Fill in the blanks with the type of scale that you hear.

1. _____   2. _____   3. _____

4. _____   5. _____   6. _____

3. You will hear eight measures of melodic dictation in the key of A harmonic minor. Fill in the blank measures with the notes and rhythms you hear. Add accidentals if needed.

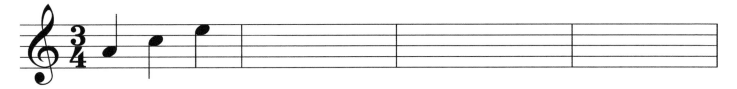

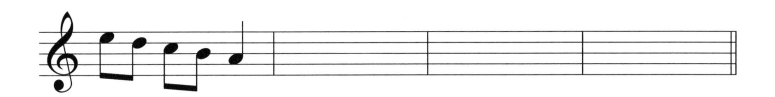

4. Circle the word that describes the texture of each musical excerpt you hear.

a. polyphonic   b. polyphonic   c. polyphonic

or   or   or

homophonic   homophonic   homophonic